C000294512

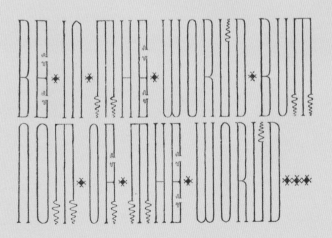

The fruit of timidity is neither gain nor loss

BE·IN·THE·WORLD·BUT
NOT·OF·THE·WORLD·

† Remember
David Guy
Barnabas
Kindersley
Sculptor
Lettercutter
Inventor
Born 11 June 1915
Died 2 Feb 1995
Husband of
Lida Helena
Lopes Cardozo
Lettercutter

The worker
is hidden in the
workshop

Cutting into the Workshop

CELEBRATING THE WORK AND LIFE
OF DAVID KINDERSLEY

Lida Lopes Cardozo Kindersley
Lottie Hoare
AND
Thomas Sherwood

CARDOZO KINDERSLEY · CAMBRIDGE 2013

First published 2013

Designed by Phil Treble, using the series layout designed by Eiichi Kono.

Photographs by Philip Moore and from the Cardozo Kindersley Archives.

The book has been set in 12 pt Emilida, a typeface designed by Lida Lopes Cardozo Kindersley, digitised by ITA Kono Design, commissioned by Timothy Guy Design for EMI. The typeface was enhanced in 2010, with many OpenType features and attention to spacing, by Eben Sorkin.

Printed in the United Kingdom at The Lavenham Press.

ISBN-13: 978-1-107-61468-0   paperback

Copies available from:
Cambridge University Press Bookshop
1 Trinity Street
Cambridge CB2 1SZ
UK

Front cover: Photography by Jürgen Röhrscheid
Inside covers: Graphic Sayings, drawn from Sufic sources – see bibliography
Frontispiece: The Workshop 2012

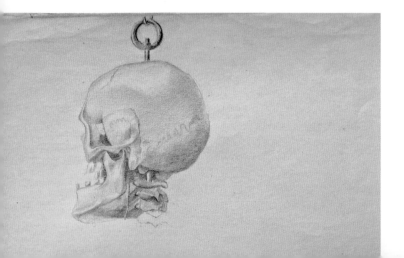

Contents

Introduction

The English-speaking world has its lettering man for the second half of the 20th century: David Kindersley's 100th birthday is coming up in 2015. Following on from 'Cutting through the Colleges' (2010), 'Cutting across Cambridge' (2011) and 'Cutting around Cambridgeshire' (2012), we complete the Cambridge University Press celebration of his Workshop with an account of the man and his times.

As to our title, we are mindful of Kingsley Amis (in Jake's Thing, 1978): 'If there's one word that sums up everything that's gone wrong since the War, it's Workshop'. We use the term throughout in its original sense of a communal place of work for artisans. There is a long history, from medieval times, to this ideal of a training ground for fine work by a master and apprentices.

The book's illustrations are largely taken from the great body of work that David Kindersley kept in his Workshop. The range is wide: stones galore of course, but also from schoolboy drawings to sculptures, and the continual experiments with new lettering forms. There is a particularly intense quest for novel alphabets in the 1960s.

From the mid-1970s David Kindersley's partnership with Lida Lopes Cardozo made each new work a joint effort. There are obvious changes in style for these last 20 years of his life. The book therefore divides naturally into two periods (written by LH, and TS). We end with a look forwards into the 21st century.

LLCK & TS

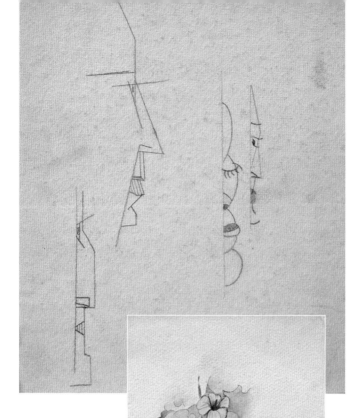

These were drawn around 1930: David was trying out modern styles but also made sensitive drawings from nature.

7

It is 18 years since I last talked with David Kindersley (1915–1995) about his memories of his letter-cutting workshop. As I sift through papers and re-read his recollections I realise that when we spoke in the early 1990s his workshop had been anchored in one location for several decades. I will attempt now to re-tell the story of how that workshop evolved. In the years prior to the conclusion of World War II David was still learning about workshops – working at lettering, drawing and carving sometimes with a group of individuals and sometimes in solitude. In the Post-War world he was thoroughly committed to working in a workshop setting. His workshop – 'David Kindersley's Workshop' from 1945 to 1995 – was nomadic in the sense that it appeared and re-appeared in different Cambridge locations but the ethos that evolved and the work that was made became interdependent in such a way that when the workshop outlived him, it did so with his guidance. I hope in the text that follows to give some sense of what the workshop meant to David Kindersley and to remember various individuals who shaped its evolution.

The workshop in 2012 – 'The Cardozo Kindersley Workshop' since 1996 – manages to be both a busy and focussed working space, and a museum to what has gone on before. I am always struck when visiting how words are everywhere and yet so often there is no need to speak. The repetitive tap of the chisel provides a sound track. Juxtapositions of words and images fill every surface. Some are obvious celebrations of the past – such as the large plastic 1960s alphabet hanging where a visitor can look through the spaces between letters and out of the window to the

The Workshop's school room as it is now.

Watercolour by Petra Gill given to David whilst he was an apprentice to her father (1934–36).

world beyond; or the intricate watercolour produced by Eric Gill's daughter Petra as a child with its rich sense of colour. Other small neat visual arrangements are practical things that belong to work today: folded blankets, small pieces of wood, bowls of walnuts to eat and tripods with small spot-lights on showing changing shadows within letter forms. Words appear not just on the letter cutting in progress but also on treasured carvings, postcards, prints and so forth. The words remind me of David Kindersley's sense of discipline: 'Hasten slowly'; 'Be still and know that I am'; 'Quiet'; 'Perfection'. I remain intrigued by the tensions that exist between the materials of craftsmanship, and the language used to communicate with those who don't have those craft skills.

David's own inner search shaped his life in ways that those around him were often unaware of and excluded from. He was influenced by the writings of Ananda Coomaraswamy who disapproved of the publication of details about people's private lives as a matter not of modesty but of principle. Coomaraswamy believed that freedom from self would come from a devotion to task where man instead of becoming preoccupied by his individual self-expression would accept himself as an instrument of creativity. Even if a strict adherence to philosophical and spiritual guidelines lay behind David's drive to work at his lettering and keep a workshop going for over forty years, he also led an earthly life. The very nature of his business meant he was dependent on good relations with the outside world. In practical terms, it was the people that he met and the opportunities that arose from these encounters that enabled him to make his work his life. The material support that came from established clients allowed him to concentrate on his lettering but also on the dedicated teaching that he provided to those around him. The working environment that he created with the help of friends, pupils and apprentices formed an essential part of his approach to life. He liked all the physical stages of making an object to go on under one workshop roof.

Ananda Coomaraswamy (1877–1947) was an art historian and curator at Boston Museum of Fine Arts. His groundbreaking studies introduced ancient Indian art and Singhalese crafts and culture to the West and explained the interconnections between art, religion, philosophy and social justice. David Kindersley considered him a fundamental influence on both Eric Gill's art and his thinking.

A workshop requires dependence on and delegation to others. This account will try to recreate an impression of how a changing group of individuals collaborated over time. Successful co-operation of groups brings the works into being. To begin, David Kindersley was born, in 1915, out of a marriage that brought together influential families. His maternal grandfather, Sir Edmund Elton, was known as the 'Potter baronet'. He had set up a pottery at the family home, Clevedon Court, in Somerset, and as an entirely self-taught potter he maintained that the nature of the clay vessel in front of him and the tools he used governed his style of decoration. He did not read books on the subject of pottery – he experimented. Even as a small child David was aware of the craftsman's work as something that could be closely integrated into the family home. Family rows meant that David did

One of the Potter baronet's pieces, heavily glazed.

David's mother: to the left pictured as a young woman; to the right three drawings made by David over the years. The fourth drawing is of his sister Ruth.

not visit his grandfather after the age of 4 but at this stage he had already framed the memory of his grandfather working in the pottery behind the main house; a seemingly peaceful retreat with steep terraced gardens stretching out beyond.

Elton's daughter, Kathleen, was married in 1902 to a man quite unlike her father. Guy Molesworth Kindersley was to be Conservative MP for Hitchin and came from a background where banking and outward convention were highly prized. David was the fifth and youngest child of his parents' union and they had been married for 13 years by the time he was born. While the social and career paths of his older siblings preoccupied his parents, he had time to busy himself making things and asking himself questions about how things were made. He would resolve the questions through working on making things – exploring the interactions between tools and materials. He watched his siblings fight battles with his parents and came to the conclusion that anger did not help. In later life he likened disruptive behaviour to a drawing taking the wrong direction.

David shunned those aspects of family life that made him uncomfortable. His father's devout and demonstrative support for the Church of England, for instance, made David wary about theatrical public display. The drama and aggression of family life overwhelmed him also and he remained uncomfortable with public anger for the rest of his life. However, other childhood memories such as the archaeological dig in the garden of their Hertfordshire family home which allowed David to witness the digging up of the inscription in capitals 'Virtus Fecit' seems to have had a profound effect. Such experiences can be seen to have sparked David's desire to keep the words and the letterforms of the past alive in the now. While part of that inscription was lost to history David was to give history back many new stone sentences.

David's father, and on the right a self-portrait.

Schooling at St Cypriot's Preparatory School in Eastbourne, and later Marlborough College, did not provide David with a community where his ingenuity or determination was understood. David recollected that art at Marlborough was taught by a colonel who would command 'One, two, three, start

The upper two drawings are self-portraits; and David drew his school friends at Marlborough College.

drawing.' One positive legacy from Marlborough College was his meeting with Rupert Mullins, who became a lifelong friend. However, the death of his much loved older brother Hallam, from a blood disease while away at school, exacerbated David's sense of mistrust about conventional education and he himself left

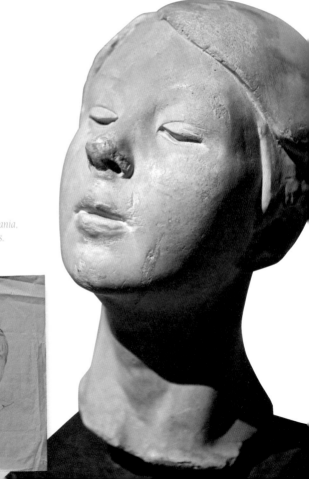

David's first love Grania, from the early 1930s.

The local policeman, a mentor who was inspiring to David.

school at the age of 15, suffering from a rheumatic illness. Convalescence brought new opportunities to experiment with carving at home in Hertfordshire. Next he went to drawing classes at the Académie Julian in Paris. David found these crowded and the communication between pupil and teacher was minimal. He missed one-to-one time with a teacher and in the long term realised the importance of this kind of dialogue and shared looking in the workshop setting.

The drawing master at the Académie Julian in Paris.

David as the conventional dashing young man; and then how he really sees himself whilst at Eric Gill's.

David then went to help out at the sculpture studios of Gilbert Ledward and Briton Rivière, and subsequently took a marble-carving job with the Induni brothers where he was required to make copies of forms modelled by established sculptors. David knew from practical experience that the shaping of one material such as clay may not look or feel convincing if exactly replicated in another material such as stone or marble. Reading Eric Gill's Art Nonsense and Other Essays (1929) reinforced David's sense that copying was not helpful: the individuals who conceived an idea should be responsible for making their vision in its final three-dimensional form. David sought out an interview with the artist and craftsman Eric Gill.

David's subsequent years spent with Eric Gill, learning directly from him and with his community of workmen, has been well documented elsewhere, so I will touch briefly on it here. David arrived at Gill's workshop in Pigotts in 1934. There was no official apprenticeship but the word apprentice is generally used to describe his role. This was his first introduction to the crafts of letter carving in stone. Gill was preoccupied with writing *The Necessity of Belief* (1936). Its call for social unity and a 'brotherhood' of men fuelled David's interest in the integration of work, family and friendship. The working conversations with Gill sparked David's lifelong interests in philosophy and faith as the driving forces behind man as a sincere, creative maker. The collaborative work of these two men took place not simply in the

An example of raised lettering by Eric Gill – a plaster cast now in the Workshop.

workshop but on site. David loved to listen to Gill's stories late at night when they were finishing carvings on a scaffold and observing the different shadows created by streetlight as opposed to sunlight. David came away from these discussions more and more convinced that it was faith of some sort that drove men on, but that the church, as a representation of institutional religion, remained a place of architectural and inscriptional interest not a spiritual necessity. David maintained a belief that Gill could respect his position but that other Roman Catholic workmen at Pigotts could not. When it came to Gill's self-congratulation that he had successfully integrated family and working life David was far more sceptical. He saw Gill as inspiring but drawn to distractions such as farming the land when he did not really

These two pictures of his were given by Eric Gill to his apprentice David.

recognise the organisation needed to rear animals. In David's view, Gill understood workshops – not agriculture.

As Gill was the senior of the two, in age and experience, the relationship between Gill and David is recorded in far more detail by David than by Gill. We can surmise, however, that Gill trusted David's total commitment to his work. As a single man the doing of his work as well as he could was his sole aim. Unlike much of Gill's workforce he had no wife or family and therefore no financial commitments. David never became a Roman Catholic so he was inevitably an outsider within the group of believers at Pigotts but he had strong friendships with some individuals regardless of religious allegiance. Eric Gill's daughter Petra, for instance, remained a lifelong friend and David was to describe her as 'the calmest most serene person I have ever met'. Petra was married to Denis Tegetmeier and they already had small children of their own. At this point Eric Gill probably saw David as a trustworthy boy rather than another man on his territory and as a result felt especially comfortable with him. David Kindersley also remembered David Jones with great affection and years later, in the 1990s, David would eat his evening meals at home, with the workshop one floor below him, and above him on the wall of his dining area, a Jones inscription.

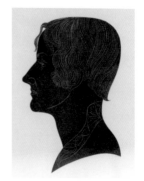

Beatrice Warde by Eric Gill.

DVGWYL·DAMASEVS
BABYRVNVED·DYÐAR
ÐEG·OVIS·RAGFYR
DVW·GWENER+
ACYNA·I·BWRIWYD
HOLL·GYMRY
YR·ILAWR·VENIT·SVMMA·DIES
ET·INELVCTABILE·TEMPVS
DARDANIÆ·PENN·DRAGON
PENN·DREIC·OED·ARNAW
PENN·ILYWELYN·DEG
DYGYN·A·VRAW·BYT·BOT
PAWL·HAEARN·TRWYDAW.
ab·hieme·añ·1282

NYT·OES·NA·XYNGOR·NA·XLO·NAC·EGOR·

The David Jones inscription.

Much of David's working life was to involve creating work which was to be placed in Christian churches. In conversation, he was happy to allow that by tradition 'Of course in England we're all Christians.' He would brush off more elaborate enquiries about his religious beliefs with a jocular retort such as 'I have never felt God needed me.' David's involvement in the Walker Group that began in the mid 1930s and was to continue with weekly meetings for the next forty years was to feed his interest in religion in a way that was not simply informative but intrinsically concerned with spiritual development. David was 'fearfully interested' in the writings of Ouspensky and Gurdjief, in the traditions of Sufism and in a search for self-realisations that went beyond our usual perceptions.

Sufism is the ancient and mystical dimension of Islam. The Sufi teacher, Idries Shah (1924–1996), published 'The Way of the Sufi' (Jonathan Cape, 1968) and this book brought the ideas, practices, sayings and riddles of Sufism to a wider audience in Britain.

David's 'Angel Torso', much influenced by Gill.

In Loving Memory

An early design by David.

24

His interest in the Walker Group started in the mid 1930s when David and his brother Edmund attended a public lecture in London. David did not initially see the Walker Group as something particularly connected with his work but he realised over time that it was to have an 'enormous effect' on his work and that it had brought him the strength and discipline he needed to run a lettering workshop. The essential aim of trying to recreate the state of mind best able to avoid the distraction of the modern world was to influence his approach to everything he did from then onwards - from his views on Gill, as we have seen above, to the conversation and advice that he gave his workshop staff in years to come. The approach to life which he gleaned from these gatherings he articulated to others but the actual activity of attending the meetings and the details of what went on there were mentioned to no one but family and very close friends. One member of the Walker Group, Phyllis Thoms, remembered David having a wonderfully distinctive voice, which she attributed to the fact that he had not been at Marlborough for long enough for his voice to be distorted by this type of schooling.

At this time David was passionate about becoming a sculptor: this beloved drawing by Henri Gaudier-Brzeska is a key to his sculptural ideal.

When David left Pigotts in 1936 his intention was to become a sculptor and he was involved with relatively few lettering commissions over the next six years.

25

A drawing of a young woman that instantly translates into stonecutting; together with a self-portrait.

He wanted to make simple figurative forms in the round, building on what he had learned from Gill while working on relief carvings. He was not yet passionate about lettering or for that matter about operating within a workshop space. He rented a remote cottage – Keeper's Cottage - near the medieval settlement of Oakhurst in Sussex. It could not be reached by road – visitors had to take a track across the fields. He lived alone there and attempted to grow his own food. The surrounding community in the Billingshurst area consisted of farm workers. David wore oiled Russian wool roll neck jumpers and blue linen shirts and kept his hair long at the sides – some contemporaries described him as looking rather as a saint would look. He became dispirited; realising that working in this way gave him no way to market his sculptures or indeed to find the means to earn a living. He buried many of the forms in the garden and decided to focus on making what people needed.

Three life drawings.

He took on lettering commissions and a part time job teaching lettering at Horsham Art School. This was the first time he was to share Gill's teaching of lettering such as he had experienced it. Vincent Lines was Principal of the Horsham Art School and it was here that David first met him and attended his life drawing classes. He enjoyed the informal atmosphere and the brightly lit 1890s building with light

Vincent Lines (1909–1968) studied at the Royal College of Art and was highly regarded by Sir William Rothenstein. He contributed a number of watercolours of the English countryside to Sir Kenneth Clark's 'Recording Britain' scheme during World War II. Richard Kindersley remembers him as a 'uniquely close' friend to David Kindersley. Lines believed that drawing and painting enabled 'deepening of conscience and seeing things which are ordinarily missed.'

27

David drawn by Vincent Lines.

Two drawings by David.

pouring in through large paned windows. He also made friends
with Donald Standing, a talented draughtsman who had won
a local authority scholarship to attend the classes although he
worked in a butcher's the rest of the week to support his mother
and siblings. David offered to take him on as a pupil but Donald
could not take the cut in wages. David felt increasingly aware
that working alone was not the way ahead. He wanted to work
with unpretentious assistants rather than to make a mark in
fashionable artistic society.

    In these years there is a clear sense that David was watching
others go about the building of a community before realising

that setting up his own workshop was the way forward. He was interested in the Cokelers Community in his nearby village of Warnham. Their official name was The Society of Dependents and they were Christian in background but also concerned with setting up co-operatives within villages. David remembered them not for their religion but because of their furniture and the fact they provided almost all that their village needed from their store and the profits from their business were used to help those who had suffered through war. He appreciated a community that looked outward to provide people with what they needed, rather than being absorbed in contemplation. He was also interested in the Bruderhof community in these years – some members of the community had fled Nazi Germany and settled in southern England.

David's friendship with Thomas Hennell, which evolved in the years before World War II, was to have a significant influence. Vincent Lines introduced the two men. Hennell was writing books in praise of the country craftsman. He looked with reverence to the precise and purposeful skills of the craftsman and the way in which they were handed on as a tradition. The respect that Hennell afforded to such abilities was to enhance David's confidence in the role of the letter cutter. He followed Hennell's belief that most conventional education should

Thomas Hennell (1903–1945) was a writer and illustrator. His publications included 'Change on the Farm' (Cambridge University Press, 1934) and 'Poems' (Oxford University Press, 1936) with wood engravings by Eric Ravilious. Hennell worked as a war artist from 1943–1945 depicting scenes in Iceland, Normandy, Holland, India and Burma. He died in mysterious circumstances after being captured by terrorists in Indonesia.

be regarded with suspicion but 'those who made things better worth troubling after' – to quote Hennell, it was understood that the guidance of such people would remain with you for life. David was fascinated by Hennell's sharp eye – his illustrations of workshops and labouring in the rural community. He never looked for short cuts and drew every tool or piece of machinery as if it could function in three dimensions.

In 1939 David married Christina Sharpe and Richard Kindersley was born that year. David took up a tenancy on a tiny Dorset Pub 'The Smiths Arms'. He did not yet know if his stance as a conscientious objector would result in his being sent to prison so he guessed that with a business to run his family could secure an income if he was absent. A second son, Peter Kindersley, was born in 1941. David continued to take lettering commissions and to work on them in the pub.

Christina, David's first wife, and their two sons Richard and Peter.

David with his children at Barton.

A sensitive drawing of David's only daughter Katie.

The Horsham area where David was based up until the outbreak of World War II was notorious for its fascist sympathies and political discussions were avoided at the Horsham Art School, because people were aware of the potential for conflict. David was averse to all conflict and believed that in all cases war was 'a total waste.' He saw the overproduction of armaments as responsible for drawing men into unnecessary battles. He took an absolutist stance as a conscientious objector and received complete exemption from War Service. With his sudden move to Dorset, he came before Judge Ernest Wethered, who was renowned for granting more unconditional exemptions in the South Western Tribunal. He was also a contemporary of David's father at Lincoln's Inn and keen on pottery but we cannot now know if those sympathies helped. Other contemporaries and protégés of Eric Gill, such as Anthony Foster and Walter Shewring made themselves available for civilian work in the war effort. Some of David's extended family was appalled by his exemption but his cousin, the film maker Sir Arthur Elton, accepted it.

David's pub tenancy in Dorset was interrupted by reorganisations at Pigotts after the death of Eric Gill in 1940. In 1942 Mary Gill and David communicated by letter and organised his return to help with the smooth running of the lettering workshop.

Sir Arthur Elton (1906–1973) was recruited by the film maker John Grierson in the 1930s and helped to pioneer documentary film making in Britain. In 1957 he became production head of the Shell Film Unit and in this role he produced a number of significant short films, which reflected his interests in aesthetics, technology and industrial development. His collection of art and artefacts was bequeathed to Ironbridge Museum in Shropshire.

The shell carved in Ketton stone was the emblem for the Shell Film Unit's movies – compare page 49.

David had shown himself capable of producing carved lettering alone without the support of a workshop team but his move back was not entirely altruistic. With a young family to support in a nation at war, the prospect of the company and connections of an established and relatively self-sufficient lettering workshop looked promising. Many of David's friends and contemporaries described this time when the threat of Hitler's invasion seemed very possible, as a point in history where 'Nobody seemed to be really dug in.'

The inhabitants of Pigotts were trying to maintain as simple a life as possible in an increasingly chaotic world. David was shocked by the lack of uniform vision in the absence of Gill. However, he enjoyed working with Denis Tegetmeier and felt that he was helpful in guiding him to transfer lettering designs onto stone. Charles Radnor who worked for Scuplture and Memorials also had an office at Pigotts (evacuated from London

Some examples of David's lettering for the Shell Film Unit.

ART
IS THAT WORK
AND THAT WAY OF WORKING
IN WHICH MAN USES
HIS FREE WILL

A civilization based upon
the doctrine of Free Will
naturally and inevitably
PRODUCES ARTISTS

IN SUCH A CIVILIZATION ALL MEN ARE ARTISTS
AND SO THERE IS NO NEED TO TALK ABOUT IT

★

THE TEXT IS FROM AN ESSAY BY ERIC GILL ENTITLED 'IDIOCY OR ILL WILL'

THE TYPE FACE IS 'MONOTYPE' PERPETUA, DESIGNED BY ERIC GILL, SERIES 239 WITH TITLING CAPITALS 258 AND BOLD 200

Printed in England for B.W by The Monotype Corporation Limited

during the war years) and he sought out commissions. The sale
of various Gill items to the United States to settle Gill's tax bills
was also ongoing during David's second residency, and perhaps
as he watched Gill's workshop and home being deconstructed
he regretted having left after a two-year period some six years
earlier. Now he was surrounded by the tapping of chisels
resounding through the beech woods and examples of Gill's
lettering everywhere, but the conversation with and presence
of his mentor was absent. For some David would always be
an outsider because he was not part of a cohesive Roman Catholic
community. David meanwhile wanted a sense of unity to come
through their shared understanding of making beautiful things.

For Christina life was not easy: a third child Katie was born
in 1943, living conditions were basic and there was no electricity.
Resident schoolmistress May Reeves was not attuned to
progressive ideas and seemed to have depended on brandishing
rulers. Peter Kindersley, the future champion of self-educating
children's non-fiction Dorling Kindersley, spent only one day
in her unruly classroom and refused to go back. Education
happened outside the classroom at Pigotts: inventing kingdoms
with fallen trees and letting tricycles go out of control on
steep hills.

Peter Kindersley with
his half-brothers Paul,
Vincent and Hallam
in 1990.

35

For all the difficulties of Pigotts during the war years,
Kindersley's technical ability in cutting letters improved during
this second period. Laurie Cribb was a positive influence. Having
so much work channelled through Sculpture and Memorials
created stylistic difficulties because people were commissioning
designs from catalogues printed in the 1930s. David was most
comfortable with secular commissions. Even if David was held
back from developing his lettering in a very conspicuous sense,
because of the tendency of clients to want work that looked like
a pastiche of Gill and Joseph Cribb from the previous decade,
he was exposed to new ways of thinking during these years.
Without Gill's conversation he began to read more. He began
to wonder what man was working for and to be fascinated by
Sufi writings. He was curious to see how words spoken and
written down as accepted truths in the past related to the very
physical work that he carried out in the present. The most vivid
connection for him was man's search for an understanding of
how the eye works and what seeing really is. David's lists of
'wants' written into a notebook in the summer of 1944 include:
'To read more', 'To give more time to psychology', 'quietness' and
'to think more simply.'

In 1945, David and a young Kevin Cribb
left Pigotts with David's wife and children.
They felt a certain pioneering enthusiasm for a
new start. David had recently purchased barns
and a farmhouse and had, along with Kevin
Cribb, been developing a lettering workshop in
these premises – known as Dales Barn – in

David Dewey, apprentice,
drawn by David.

Apprenticeship alphabet painted by David Dewey.

the village of Barton, Cambridgeshire. David Dewey joined the workshop as an apprentice in 1946 and David Parsley in 1950. David Holgate and David's son Richard Kindersley joined as apprentices in 1955. So many people who came across David in these years remember him as a natural teacher: incredibly kind and encouraging. He never talked down to people and those around him seemed to relax into their work. Many who spent even short periods at the workshop speak of his ability to introduce them to their own capabilities and to a way of life that they could build on after they had left. David Holgate and Richard Kindersley remembered also how much they learned from tea break discussions where David Kindersley was keen that apprentices understood his views, ideas and integrity of thinking.

A drawn letterhead for Dales Barn Workshop.

a

ABCDEFGHIJKL
MNOPQRSTUVW
XYZ & abcdefghijk
lmnopqrstuvwxyz

An early David Kindersley alphabet – slate cut.

Life at Dales Barn offered vivid reminders of Gill's domestic and work setting: the workshops and cottage facing in on each other; the simplicity of the kitchen with its Windsor chairs, its neat rows of pots, the occasional picture of an alphabet on an otherwise white and uncluttered wall; and the temporary residents, teachers and apprentices housed in caravans. There was a sense that these people had something to offer each other that was important enough to go without the ordinary. However, David was not a man who was satisfied to copy in any aspect of his work or life. He was excited by new events and ideas in post-war England and he was also aware that there was much that Gill had not achieved in his lettering. The debt David felt he owed to Gill was much more to

38

Maquette for the Corpus Christi College column in Grantchester churchyard. The material is clunch: Cambridgeshire's only stone; it cuts readily but breaks easily.

do with his way of working than his lettering itself. Ralph Beyer recalls his excitement at finding that lettering was the priority at Dales Barn, after Pigotts under Gill, where lettering had only been one of various pursuits.

Dales Barn housed no religious imagery and there were no religious rituals to break up the day. Work and the workshop were sacred without needing to be conspicuously linked to the Christian tradition. In conversations with those who knew David's first workshop in its own right in its early years small

An exhibition panel showing (top right) the Corpus Christi 'pelican in its piety'. This 1950 Portland stone column is 3 metres high – the bird's wingspan 61 cm.

visual memories recur: wrens perched on easels,
the smell of spilt tea cooking on the top of the
oil heater, eating sandwiches round a brazier
in the darkened barn workshop in winter, and
unravelling Bernard Leach's pale green glazed
beakers from their tissue when the cottage next to
the farmhouse was ready to move into.

One of the greatest assets at Dales Barn
was space. Only the Kindersley family lived
there permanently so there was not the feeling
of being crowded in amongst other families.
The workshop, housed as it was in long barns
that were open on one side, provided plenty of
workroom and enabled cars and deliveries to be
driven straight in. Lucie Rie visited once when
in Cambridge for a craft exhibition and she was
very taken with the workshop, describing it:
'... strange and beautiful barn workshops with
all these magnificent views.' Dales Barn had
a thriving vegetable garden, attended to in part
by the Kindersley children, but there were no
farm animals.

When David moved to Barton in the mid 1940s there was no one else in the Cambridgeshire area working in the same way. David's arrival came to the attention of the University Printer, Brooke Crutchley, who had known and admired Gill. David was patently a kindred spirit when it came to knowledge and respect for the English lettering revival of the previous fifty years. David saw his meeting with Brooke Crutchley as a turning point that led to so many opportunities.

The letter cutter Ralph Beyer's arguments as to why David's lettering was so well received by Cambridge University Press are very helpful to our understanding. David shared the typographical concerns of Crutchley and John Dreyfus but he could translate these concerns to lettering in stone without copying typefaces (see also page 57). His totally unselfconscious understanding of the materials with which he worked meant that an observer could appreciate his sharp eye and his precision, and yet his lettering always belonged to stone and slate and never looked like a page from a book.

At John Dreyfus's instigation, a group including Brooke Crutchley, Will and Sebastian Carter, Jack Goodison, Raymond Lister, John Peters, David Peace and David Kindersley would meet up on the first Friday of every month for lunch at the Green

Brooke Crutchley (1907–2003) was the University Printer at Cambridge University Press from 1946–1974, a period which saw huge changes in printing technology. He read Classics and English at Trinity Hall in the 1920s and was elected a fellow in 1951. He was highly respected for his consistency of purpose and his respect for typographical tradition. The Kindersley work for the Press is now in its seventh decade.

The work done for Cambridge University Press also led David to Letraset (see page 73).

Man pub in Trumpington. The general aim of the discussions was sometimes described as 'Putting University lettering to rights' although the commissions that evolved from these meetings often went far beyond the realms of Cambridge University.
This informal gathering probably engendered more successful work contacts and fruitful exchanges of ideas than the Designer Craftsmen Society, which was later expressly set up in Cambridge for that purpose.

John Dreyfus (1918–2002) was a printer, typographer and historian of private press publications.
He read Economics at Trinity College, Cambridge, and was Assistant University Printer at Cambridge University Press from 1949–1955.
He then took over from Stanley Morison as typographical adviser to the Monotype Corporation and held the post until 1982.

David's original drawing for street lettering.

The trial sign for Trumpington Street had each letter carefully cut out by hand and stuck onto the painted wooden board. Red Lion Square was the first example cast in metal.

The many Ministry of Transport regulations applying to street lettering, with some examples of available typefaces.

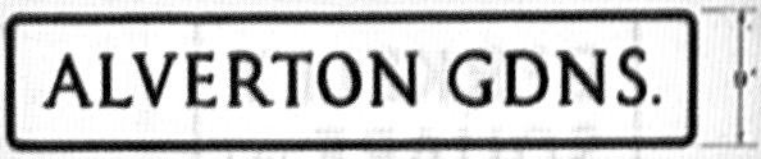

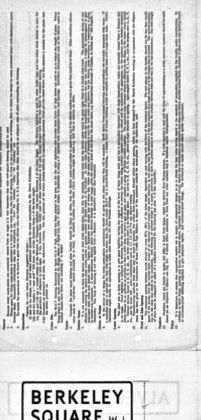

ALVERTON GDNS.
9"

FIG. I KINDERSLEY — 3½"

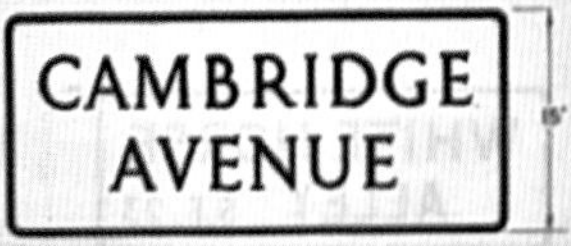

CAMBRIDGE
AVENUE
15"

FIG. II KINDERSLEY — 3½"

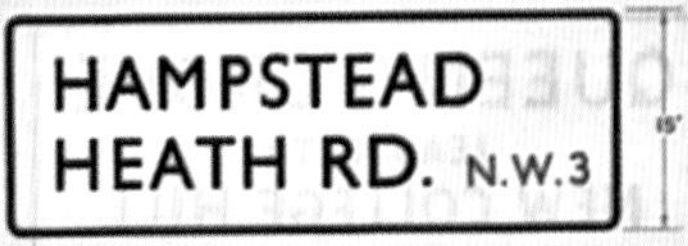

HAMPSTEAD
HEATH RD. N.W.3
15"

FIG. III GILL (½)—3½" & 2"

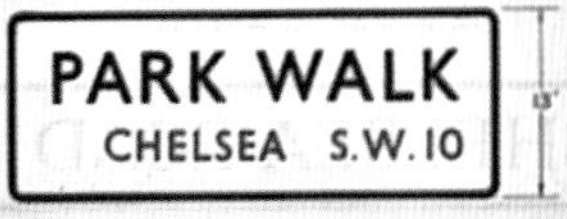

PARK WALK
CHELSEA S.W.10
13"

FIG. IV GILL (½)—3½" & 2"

BERKELEY
SQUARE W.1
15"

FIG. V M.O.T. (i) — 4" & 2"

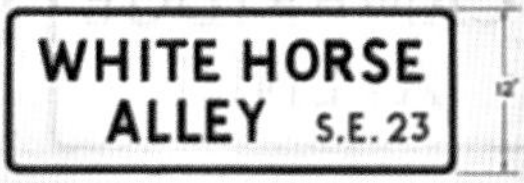

WHITE HORSE
ALLEY S.E.23
12"

FIG. VI M.O.T. (i) — 3" & 2"

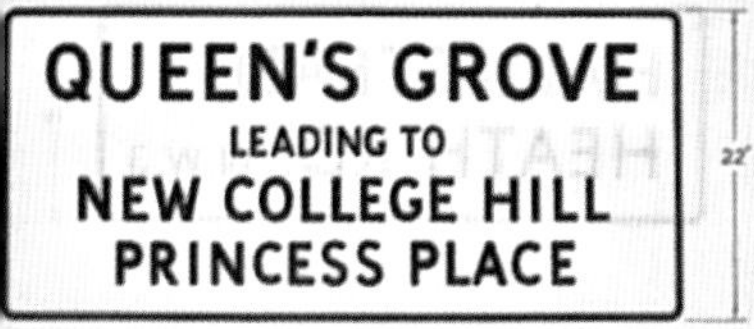

QUEEN'S GROVE
LEADING TO
NEW COLLEGE HILL
PRINCESS PLACE
22"

FIG. VII M.O.T. (i) — 4,3 & 2"

CHELSEA ROAD
9"

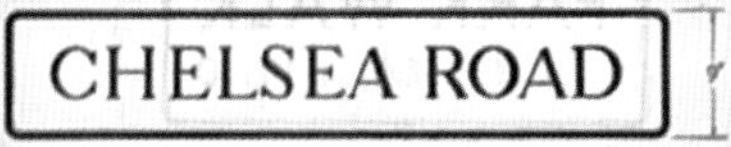

FIG. VIII CASLON OLD FACE — 3½"

ABC
DEFGHIJKL
abcdefghijklm
MNOPQRST
nopqrstuvwx
UVWXYZ&
yz & abcdefghijklm
1234 56789
nopqrstuvwxyz Kindersley 51

A Workshop sample dated 1951 –
slate cut, 46 × 32 cm.

manufacture, *man-ū-fakt'yar, v.t.* to make, originally by hand, now usu. by machinery: to produce unintelligently in quantity.

Slate for the Haymarket Design Centre: this dictionary quotation was not received with immediate enthusiasm by industry.

David looked on his pub lunches with friends who cared about lettering and design as something of an education. He had never had anything to do with a large printing house before, his experience of printing having been previously confined to his irritation with René Hague at Pigotts, for what he saw as his poaching Gill away from letter cutting. This printing world did not distract David from the running of his own workshop. He enjoyed hearing about lettering from engravers and printers who had to put it to different uses than he had. Their talk fed his fascination with letterforms, legibility and the application of spacing to all forms of lettering. David liked such occasions where he could share his love of work with other practical people and where small talk was irrelevant.

David also made work contacts in Cambridge through his teaching at the Cambridge College of Arts & Technology. He ran an evening class in letter cutting at this establishment for ten years. He had thoroughly enjoyed his pre-war teaching at Horsham Art School but perhaps because he now had the experience of running a workshop to compare it to he didn't find his teaching work in the 1940s and 1950s so inspiring. He preferred helping apprentices in the workshop 'precisely because it was work.' With his two-hour class every Tuesday, David met with pupils who had often been told to attend by their fee-paying employers. They signed up to placate their firms but they felt none of the responsibility that David was used to finding from his apprentices. David remembered them preferring to go and play ping-pong despite their name being signed up for lettering. There was something about the idea that one was there to 'learn' rather than 'work' which David found rather distasteful. It reminded him too much of the institution of school.

Will Carter (1912–2001) was a letterpress printer, typographer and carver who had started his own private press as a school boy. In 1949 he dedicated himself full time to The Rampant Lions Press. Highly regarded books included a project that William Morris and Edward Burne-Jones made blocks for but never printed: 'The Story of Cupid and Psyche' (1974).

Gill had learnt letter-cutting at night school and David had some faint hope that one day a pupil would come along with the commitments and concentration required for letter-cutting who simply had not yet had the good fortune to meet people who could help him make this his work. If David found much of his teaching at the Tech unrewarding, the part he played in shaping the future of one pupil, Will Carter, certainly made up for this. Will Carter described how he spent years working full time at Heffers talking about how he was going to change his working life and concentrate on running a press, yet the date for change was never specified. Will gave David the credit for

inspiring him to actually take the necessary leap into the unknown with Rampant Lions Press as well as teaching him to cut letters. The example

This Portland stone was used as the Institute's emblem in its films, and later returned to the Workshop (as the Shell Film Unit did with David's shell – see page 32).

of David Kindersley who was creating a successful working life for himself without belonging to any institution was a source of encouragement to many in those years.

Besides the apprentices, others also helped in the 1950s Dales Barn workshop. Wendy Westover and Geoffrey Clarke helped particularly with drawings and Ralph Beyer and Keith Bailey with cutting workshop commissions. Keith Bailey had come from the City and Guilds Art School in London and Kindersley would grimace at his eighteenth century letter designs favoured by the head, Sharpington. Lettering was discussed in the workshop: Margaret Andrews, an art student working during the early years at Dales Barn, remembers Sunday afternoons spent arguing about the best way to do a Y with Ys being drawn all over the back of a door to prove a point. However, Will Carter recollected that lettering was examined more through drawing and cutting than through conversation.

David was opposed to what he saw as unnecessary styling in the design of various objects – cars being a case in point. Those who knew him in these years describe how he had a rather studied way of bringing things down to earth. He would tease those who favoured anything too flashy – Jaguars, for example, were compared to sucked sweets. Gertrude Horsley, a friend from the Designer Craftsmen Society, queried the styling in David's own choice of vehicles and suggested that his Messerschmitt bubble car gave the impression that it would belong to someone flighty and irresponsible.

David was interested in the ideas of progressive educationalists when it came to the education of his own small children and as a result he set up a small school at Dales Barn. He admired the local education officer Henry Morris and had met and been inspired by Herbert Read and his book Education Through Art. Read recommended to David interested students or teachers who might want to be involved with his project. Some teachers spent

Henry Morris (1889–1962) was chief education officer for Cambridgeshire from 1922–1954. He believed that education should be a lifelong process. He founded the Village Colleges, where secondary education and community education were integrated and agricultural areas benefitted from a centre for cultural and social activity. His friends described him as having no formal religion but observed that 'the possibility of full and complete living was his religion'.

A David doodle.

their time at Dales Barn teaching the children in the morning in the schoolroom and learning lettering themselves in the afternoon in the workshop. David's excitement about Read's ideas on education for children stemmed from their having a clear relationship with the workshop tradition. The workshop tradition predated the idea of 'childhood' and originally offered committed young people the chance to work.

David was interested in A. S. Neill's views on education but he did not feel that children should be offered such a degree of freedom. David favoured teaching that developed from proposals instigated by the children themselves. Richard Kindersley remembers his early schooling at Dales Barn as a time when he never felt he was being cheated. Margaret Angus took much of the responsibility for teaching the children and her work remained vivid in

Two examples of tiles by Margaret Angus (Maggie Berkowitz).

their minds. The Kindersley children had been reading about mining and wanted to dig a tunnel. They then worked with the Cambridgeshire clay they had dug up, sieving it and adding water until they could work with it making models. The project involved the children at every stage and they built a sawdust kiln in which they could fire their work. They also grew their own wheat – taking responsibility for harvesting, threshing, cutting and flailing. David wanted the children to face the repetitive and dreary aspects of the work. Under Read's guidance David ensured that the children had space for their own imagery without copying and being overawed by the work of adults. He wanted the children to make things that they did not have any conscious idea where they came from, and without stopping to examine their influences and sources. No distinctions between art and craft were suggested to the children either. The making of anything by hand – whether painting or preparing wheat to make flour – such activities were portrayed as work to be got on with without hierarchical distinctions. By the time they were twelve the children were allowed into the workshop regularly and Richard Kindersley remembers carving an owl out of clunch. They had occasionally spent time there when they were younger – setting up model villages and toy railway lines around the stones.

Kindersley still did not see his workshop as the only place where he would learn. During holidays with the ceramicist Bernard Leach he had moments of wondering whether to go and spend time at St Ives learning pottery techniques from him. He liked the idea of single-mindedly applying himself to another craft in order to expand his understanding of working with natural materials. However, responsibilities to his family and clients came first and he did not find time for this imagined education. David and Christina divorced in the early 1950s and this resulted in Dales Barn being sold but the workshops being rented back so the Workshop itself did not relocate. After the divorce, Richard and Peter went on at boarding school in Hertfordshire and then Norwich, and Katie was at day school

Teapot by Bernard Leach – all David's day-to-day crockery was made by him.

David cutting at the Madingley American Cemetery; at the height of this massive task the whole Workshop was engaged for a year. It focussed David's mind on how important it was to train people for taking on such large commissions. Even so, he did not have enough manpower for cutting the names on the walls of the Tablets of the Missing; these were machine-tooled. The Workshop concentrated on lettering and maps for the Visitors' Building, together with the three Portland stone eagles.

in Harston. Richard Kindersley remembers posting back to his father letters he was busy drawing at boarding school.

David Kindersley was busy with large Cambridge commissions for much of the 1950s. The Trinity College Chapel war memorial inscriptions began in 1951 and the commissions at Madingley American Cemetery preoccupied the Workshop through to 1960. There are detailed descriptions in our Cambridge University Press publications 'Cutting through the Colleges' (2010, pp.98–99) and 'Cutting around Cambridgeshire' (2012, pp.55–59). War memorial projects provided tasks that were technically interesting, as well as a steady income for the Workshop; but David also craved for more time to experiment with lettering. He worked as an adviser to the Shell Film Unit from 1949 to 1958 (see pages 32–33), and took an increasing

Portland stone sample letter for the large war memorial in Trinity College Chapel, Cambridge (1951, 23 × 20 cm letter).

interest in rolling film titles and animations created with lettering and lines. Richard Kindersley remembers how Saul Bass's famous title sequence for the film 'The Man with the Golden Arm' (1955) impressed David. It featured animated white on black paper cut-outs. Collaborations between designers and new technologies appealed to David, and he believed that had Gill lived to see the post-war world he would have embraced further technological changes.

A marked shift took place in David's thinking between the early 1940s and the early 1950s. At Pigotts David had resented that René Hague's Print Shop took attention away from the letter-cutting workshop. However, once settled in Cambridge he began to adopt the view that all the crafts should support each other,

Facsimile of a slate in Birmingham Public Library, with David's homage below. There is a direct line of great lettercutting from the renowned John Baskervill(e) and his typeface into the 20th century of Eric Gill and David Kindersley. Lettercutting and typeface design are closely connected – the 21st century Workshop knows the shoulders it stands on.

and that excellent printing helped to ensure the continuance of high standards in craft and design. It was his conversations with Cambridge University Press printers, such as Brooke Crutchley and John Dreyfus (see pages 42–43), that won David round; as he wrote in his autobiographical notes, recalling his first meeting with Brooke Crutchley, 'Life transformed'. The letter cutter Ralph Beyer later observed that David's lettering was so well received by Cambridge University Press because David could translate the typographical concerns of Crutchley and Dreyfus without ever copying or being overshadowed by typefaces. Beyer credited him with an unselfconscious understanding of the materials with which he worked: such that his lettering always belonged to its situation – whether it be stone, slate, plastic, paper, or glass.

Book plates are another good lettering tradition, continuing in the Workshop.

After World War II there were campaigns to encourage art schools to develop subjects that could be used in industry. Collaboration with industry became a moral issue – the wood engraver John Farleigh argued that craftsmen who refused to design for machine production at a time when three million were unemployed were without social conscience. This concern to link art school training with industry led to an invitation for David to run an incised lettering class at the Cambridge College of Art & Technology between 1945–1955. He enjoyed meeting other staff as well as students. The sign-writer Bert Le Q Winterton ran a painting and decorating class at the college. David credited him with teaching him a good deal about heraldry through informal discussions. David always valued shared stories and insights, and saw such guidance as just as important, if not more important, than direct instruction.

Two of these slate paperweights can also be seen on the opposite page.

A corner in the Workshop, showing a fashion label designed by David in the 1970s.

59

Hand & Machine is an experiment with mobile concrete blocks. They show David's obsession with finding the optical centre of each letter. This is marked by a vertical line, and it denotes the optical, not mathematical centre.

David was instrumental in setting up *The Designer Craftsmen Society* in the 1950s, along with the calligrapher Gertrude Horsley and others. It promoted the crafts through a small shop in Newnham village, Cambridge. The aim was to promote and improve fine craftsmanship and to encourage greater public recognition of well-made objects. The society evolved from discussions at lettering classes that Kindersley was running at the Cambridge College of Art & Technology.

David's own design for the Crafts Centre gallery in Hay Hill, London, was produced in 1951 around the time of the Festival of Britain. His first version was rejected on the basis that using rustic Roman lettering was inappropriate and that a sign in an urban setting must make the crafts look at home in a city. The architect's brief for Hay Hill had insisted that restrained elegance must be conveyed throughout the whole show room and exterior, so that the crafts could hold their own in this urban setting. In

contrast, the Designer Craftsmen shop, in Cambridge, deliberately aimed to be proud of rural crafts, as well as encompassing crafts that were mechanically reproduced such as printing and book jackets. The Designer Craftsmen also upheld that art and craft were integrated, and that a line could not be easily drawn between the two.

The Designer Craftsmen shop in Newnham, Cambridge, came to the attention of the cartoonist Ronald Searle. He produced an illustration of gleeful local barbers excited by the new trade of trimming craftsmen's beards while they queued for their pots to be assessed by the society. In

The Crafts Centre was not easy with David's first sign, gilded on wood. They wished for something more traditional and British: the final slate.

63

an age of austerity there were some
difficulties convincing the public about
whether the crafts belonged to the world of
luxuries or should focus, as David believed,
on producing useful, affordable things that were
needed in a community. The Designer Craftsmen shop venture
was generally well received and did much to promote the local
craftspeople. It also drew praise from non-local members such
as Bernard Leach and Lucie Rie who agreed to exhibit in its
premises. David loved the delicacy of Rie's work, which he found

*The workshop's mantelpiece: a pair of marble candleholders,
turned on the Workshop lathe.*

so demonstrative of the potter's process. When the Designer Craftsmen expanded and moved to King's Parade a dependence on volunteer staff worked less well, and in 1958 the premises became a branch of Henry Rothschild's Primavera instead. Primavera had begun as an independent craft shop in Sloane Street, London, in the late 1940s. David enjoyed the friendships that developed at crafts societies, but he found the politics and intrigue that these gatherings entailed a distraction from the making of things – by hand, in peace and quiet. In a lecture at Maryland College, Woburn, in 1975 he advised his audience: 'Make friends with your clients and stay out of the craft world'.

Bernard Leach (1887–1979) was a potter and writer. Inspired by his etching teacher, Frank Brangwyn, he spent time living in Japan and became fascinated by the unity between the traditions of the East and the West. Lucie Rie (1902–1995) was a Viennese potter who fled to London in 1938 to escape Nazism. She established her own reputation in the late 1940s with her stoneware and porcelain. She became a lifelong friend of Bernard Leach and they both had a profound influence on British studio pottery.

In 1957 David married Barbara Pym Eyre Petrie. The Dales Barn buildings had been sold but the Workshop was rented back, so in terms of letter cutting there was no change of site in these years. David and Barbara lived in Linton, and putting a distance between the Workshop and home life was significant in the view of Richard Kindersley who worked at the Workshop in the 1950s and early 1960s. He noticed that his father now had more time to draw and experiment with lettering once he was based in Linton, and could go home to an environment that was not so closely linked to the demands of his clients. Richard remembered his father's conscious discipline that he would often attempt to turn sad and difficult situations around and see them as potential opportunities. While in many ways it had been easier for his home and Workshop to be based on one site, David took advantage of the possibility of more private time to reflect on and experiment with lettering designs. Richard suggests that he reached back to 19th century influences in this period. David also reflected on 20th century influences that had inspired him over the decades. He had seen an Arts Council exhibition of Ben Shahn's work in London in 1947 and later very much enjoyed the publication of 'Love and Joy about Lettering' (1963, Grossman, New York).

Ben Shahn (1898–1969) was a graphic artist of Lithuanian descent who grew up in New York. He was interested in social realist depictions of the world around him. He used both Hebrew and Roman lettering as expressive devices in his posters and book illustrations. He integrated lettering and images in a thoughtful, playful manner. He hoped to inspire social change through his work.

Elisabeth Frink and David worked at the Curwen Press together; some of Frink's prints came to appear on the back of David's & vice versa.

Barbara Petrie portrait of David.

*Lid of a slate box for David's
second wife, Barbara.*

David also took a renewed interest in sculptural objects during the 1960s. Richard remembers how David was intrigued by plain, undecorated stone bowls in the Egyptian section of the British Museum. The way in which the line at the top of the bowl interplayed with the shape of the bowl fascinated him. David bought a heavy-duty lathe: the Workshop began to experiment with making bowls from alabaster, Hopton Wood stone and other marbles.

David was an avid pipe smoker; in 1966 Kevin Cribb and David Parsley made him this ashtray, of Hopton Wood stone.

David started to experiment with type design and in 1961 Monotype issued the Octavian typeface, which he had designed with Will Carter (see page 48). The spacing of letters

Many bowls were turned on the Workshop's lathe, made of various kinds of stone.

Monotype Octavian designed by David Kindersley and Will Carter.

preoccupied David increasingly, and his intense fascination with it sometimes led to tensions within the Workshop: when the work of letters cut in stone needed intense engagement but other projects were competing for David's attention. Designing motorway signs for the Ministry of Transport brought fresh challenges about how to achieve maximum legibility for drivers viewing the signs from different angles. The Workshop, including David Holgate, helped David experiment with the evolution of an optical spacing machine, which could recreate the position of lettering on signs and in print to give the best legibility. This exploration was the beginning of a journey in spacing, which

Monotype Corporation developed from Tolbert Lanston's experimental work with printing type. His hot metal typecasting machine was patented in 1896. By the 1920s Monotype was issuing new typefaces and revised historic typefaces under the guidance of Stanley Morison. Prominent type designers included Eric Gill, David Kindersley, Jan Van Krimpen, Beatrice Warde and Hermann Zapf.

resulted in David's computer program *Logos* in the 1980s. This venture also led David into working as a consultant to Letraset from 1964–1988.

Brooke Crutchley recalls in his autobiography 'To Be a Printer' (1980, Bodley Head) that David Kindersley was called in to advise on lettering for the outside of the new Cambridge University Press buildings in 1963. An adaptation of a design by Hermann Zapf known as 'Melior' was selected, and as 'Meliorissimo' became, in Crutchley's words, 'a symbol of their

Motorway Signs became necessary in Great Britain when the first motorway was opened in 1958. David Kindersley designed an alphabet for use on motorway signs. He proposed that serifed capital letters would be most effective and that such capital letters would be legible when smaller, therefore avoiding large ugly boards that marred the landscape. The Ministry of Transport did not adopt his designs.

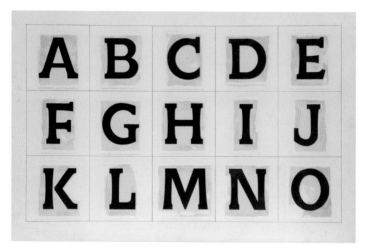

This stage of motorway letter design shows what happens when everything is concentrated on legibility, not necessarily elegance.

A big battle was fought over legibility for motorway signs; David's arguments winning hands down. However, the diktat of fashion ruled for Jock Kinnear's American-inspired lower case letters.

71

chinA		Jam		treaSure
Apple		Lion		Tree
fAther		Man		THree
Angel		Nest		moTHer
Author		luNG		dUE
Bed		On		Up
Cat		bOOk		Van
CHair		fOOd		Window
Doll		OUt		WHeel
EEl		tOE		seX
Egg		OIl		Yellow
Finger		Pig		Zoo · iS
Girl		Red		the
Hat		biRd		…ed
tIE		Soap		…ing
Ink		SHip		and

Pitman phonetic alphabet.

new identity'. This design was found on the facade and doors of the new Cambridge University Press building, and also on the livery for the delivery vans, and on letterheads. This work is all in 'Cutting across Cambridge' (2011, Cambridge University Press, pp.67–71).

Meliorissimo was used in many materials throughout Cambridge University Press, from plexiglass to Letraset. And Letraset adopted David's spacing for their commercial products; they supported him in his spacing research for many years.

In 1966 David sold a drawn and painted alphabet, based on rustic Roman lettering, to Carol Hogben, Deputy Keeper of the Circulation Department at the Victoria & Albert Museum. This vote of confidence encouraged David to experiment further. The following year brought an opportunity, which enabled him to think about what he might do if he was freed from the

responsibilities of commissioned work. In 1967 he was appointed Senior Research Fellow at the William Andrews Clark Memorial Library, Los Angeles; and here he helped to organize and exhibit the Eric Gill collection. He also met the librarian and critic Lawrence Clark Powell (1906–2001) and developed a lasting friendship. A revival of interest in Eric Gill's work in the mid-1960s encouraged David to reflect on Gill's influence on his own approach to running a workshop. Simultaneously David was excited by contemporary lettering that he saw in America, and he felt compelled to explore the relationship between imaginative

and traditional letterforms. David's recollections of his early training were also published in Los Angeles: 'Mr Eric Gill' (1967, Ward Ritchie Press). Further visits to California and opportunities to lecture on Eric Gill at the Gleeson Library occurred in the next decade.

John Dreyfus believed that the vivid, new environment of California, the sunshine, bright colours and the neon lettering used on buildings were all factors that combined to unleash a whole body of creative work from David. With this era of alphabets David was clearly fascinated by how the letters could all interact and work together homogeneously within clearly

*One of the huge excitements of David's new alphabets
was that any material could be used, at any size.
Each alphabet was given its own name.*

defined boundaries. However jagged or zigzagging the letters
became, they still cooperated without any one letter dominating.
Dreyfus reflected on what he saw as David's 'joyous' and
'liberating' work in lettering:

> In all his work, diversity of material and design is
> paradoxically matched by a strong feeling of unity,
> stemming from his mastery of spacing, and to this coupled
> a genius for evolving a design which when finished appears
> to be the only and inevitable solution to the problem posed by
> site and subject (1957, *Penrose Annual*).

77

Versal lower-case

Lombardic

Calligraphic

1900

Stick boustrophedon

Versal capitals

English

Ligature

Op.

Engravers

Boustrophedon inscription

Reed

Lower-case capitals

Shatter boustrophedon

Flourish

Arabic numerals

Vertical

Classic

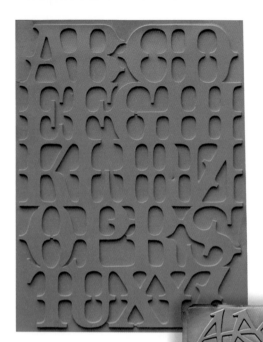

Christopher Skelton at the
Skelton Press helped David
to bring these alphabets
to a wider audience with
two beautiful Private Press
publications: 'Variations
on the Theme of 26 Letters'
(1969) and 'Graphic
Sayings' (1972). Christopher
Skelton was a modest and
dedicated collaborator when
producing these books, and
David really enjoyed working
with him. The Folio Society

*Two examples of vacuum-formed plastic
alphabets, and individual N & R; David
hoped that they could be of architectural use.*

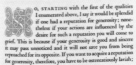

Charles Ede, founder of the Folio Society, commissioned David in 1970 to draw the initial letters for each chapter of 'The Prince' by Niccolo Machiavelli. They were derived from those in 'Hypnerotomachia Poliphili' printed by Aldus Manutius in 1499.

exhibited a series of David's giant plastic alphabets in 1969 and the Victoria & Albert Museum bought two complete sets of 18 alphabets in that year. If California had sparked a visual exuberance in David's work, the word-play and humour which is explored in 'Graphic Sayings' forms a tribute to the Sufi teacher Idries Shah. David also loved Idries Shah's publication 'The Book of The Book' (1969). Within the serious looking leather binding is a book of nothing but blank white pages.

The Moving Finger
Moves on: nor all y
Shall lure it ba
Nor all your Tears

David wanted to reflect the meaning of Homer's saying on this dove grey marble.
He commented that when you experiment you do crazy things; and then little by
little they creep into commissioned work, making it more varied and colourful.

ites; and, having writ,
r Piety nor Wit
to cancel half a Line,
sh out a Word of it.

Raised letters on slate, with the background painted off-white – another experiment with letter forms and materials.

David's work in Los Angeles in 1967 coincided with the Workshop moving to a new location, a medieval building in Cambridge city known as Chesterton Tower. Richard Kindersley, David Holgate and others had moved on from the Workshop, and the sorting out of materials in David's absence led to some accidental losses from his own archives – to his distress all his paintings were destroyed during the move.

For all his creative adventures outside the Workshop in the 1950s and 1960s, David still greatly valued working with a

*Two zinc plates for printing onto very thin Japanese paper;
they are not reversed, so that each saying is seen clearly right
through the paper.*

*group who knew each other's working practices well; and who
could cooperate to ensure that commissions were transformed
from ideas voiced to completed inscriptions. He hoped that every
possible stage was conducted and watched over within the
Workshop. By keeping as many processes – drawing, masoning,
carving, painting, gilding – under one roof, he could oversee that
all appropriate energies had been focussed on the ideal aimed at.
David's own Workshop became vital to his personal search for
greater enlightenment. The books beside his bed – Ouspensky's
'New Model of the Universe' (1931) and Pierre Teilhard de
Chardin's 'The Future of Man' (1964) – might have inspired
him to think deeply about the world around him; but it was
the immediate demands of a working community, which could
share stories and focus collectively on shared making, that had
the most powerful effect on him.*

LH

It is 1976: David Kindersley is a well-known senior figure in the lettering world. He is 61 years old, and in reflective mood, surveying the luggage accrued over the decades. He has achieved a great deal; his fame has not brought him riches. The Workshop, now at Chesterton Tower in Cambridge, is facing a rent increase. And he is married to Barbara Petrie, a painter who is unwell. The future is altogether uncertain. He is thinking of retiring from running the Workshop.

There is one small but insistent alarm bell ringing in these plans for an orderly withdrawal from the battlefield. To explore it we have to double back two years into Holland 1974.

At the Royal Academy in The Hague there is a 20 year old student of graphic design, Lida Lopes Cardozo. Her teacher Gerrit Noordzij has told her of 'a fantastic guy in Cambridge' whom he met at a conference in 1973, with other luminaries like Hermann Zapf. 'If you really want to know about lettering, you have to seek out David Kindersley'.

A stone carved by Gerrit Noordzij. Lida's teacher who was instrumental in directing her toward David.

David in Warsaw, by Lida

Two experimental pyrex glass bowls using platinum leaf and bronze powder.

86

Lida finds out that there will be a conference in Warsaw organized by the A TypI (Association Typographique Internationale), in the early autumn of 1975. DK is expected to attend, and so she signs up for it. After strip searches at the border (this is Eastern bloc Poland 1975) she eventually makes it to the huge exhibition hall in Warsaw, and has DK pointed out to her. Boldly she marches up and says 'I'm Lida from Holland'. He says 'I hate things almost perfect'. But he was looking at an exhibit, not Lida. For a moment, everything was at rest, free and immortal.

But what follows is a cold shoulder, among the plentiful Polish drinking sessions. 'Can I come and be an apprentice' is met with 'No – I'm winding down at age 60 and handing over – if you're ever in England you can come and see me'.

By the end of October 1975 Lida has an appointment with DK. She sails to England with her mother. The eagerly awaited late morning meeting at the Workshop in Cambridge is half spoilt by a nosebleed, then a lunch foursome with Harold Hunter (gold beater), then 3 pm departure. DK is his charming self, and entirely non-committal.

Lida bombards Cambridge with letters from The Hague, putting her intense enthusiasm for this work. They are each unanswered. In 1976 Reading University runs a summer conference with a workshop by DK on letter spacing – a Dutch girl signs up again. Her last two days there are in DK's class, and she is insistent: an apprenticeship in Cambridge please! At the end of the conference there is a party on the Thames, and DK relents. 'I'm going on a lecture tour in the United States in the autumn – if you want to help with the photography for that you can come then – you can do photographs?'

By August 1976 Lida is at the Workshop in Cambridge, unpaid, in a bedsit, and working on material for 3 lectures on Eric Gill, the Workshop and letter spacing.

Every apprenticeship has to begin with drawing out and cutting a capital alphabet – this is Lida's, in Hopton Wood stone.

It is largely evening work, with some excursions to other places like Gill's old workshop in Buckinghamshire. And then the slides are all done, and DK is off to Heathrow with them. 'If you're still here when I return...'. And flies away for two months. Lida stays on at the Workshop, and cuts her first alphabet.

Painting of Paul Lopes Cardozo, the Dutch cytologist (signed D. Stapel 1995). Lida's father funded her apprenticeship, saying 'if you really think this is it, OK, go ahead, it's a one-off'.

When David had finished drawing Keats' Lamia, Lida cut it in yellow magnesium limestone. And that Woodhouse quarry is now closed, with the supermarket on top; David's pithy comment was 'hadn't we better leave some of the good stuff for the next generation?'.

Then Christmas 1976, and things have moved on. DK had returned from the States to find Lida indeed still there, stubbornly settled in the Workshop. So he accepts that, has started working with her, and offered an apprenticeship next year at £15 a week. But other money matters suddenly dominate. Chesterton Tower's rent is to go up by 900%, later negotiated to 300%. The old Victorian school at 152 Victoria Road is on the market; DK is backed by Lida in determining that this is the way forward for the Workshop, much against the will of the 3 assistants. How is the money to be raised when the master already has an overdraft, runs a hire/purchase car, and lives in a house owned by his wife?

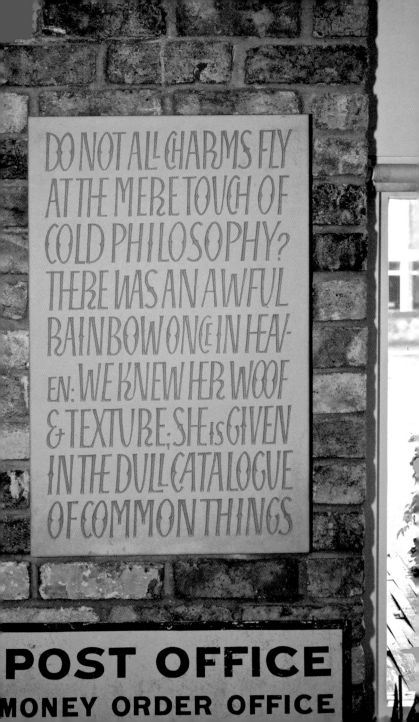

The first 9 months of 1977 are a whirl. Lida the apprentice also takes over the billing of the Workshop, clients are asked to pay a third of the cost for their work in advance, there is a grant, a bank loan, and the goodwill for Chesterton Tower is worth something. All at once buying and refurbishing 152 Victoria Road for the new Workshop looks achievable, and Lida is sleepless.

In the autumn of 1977 they are ready for the move. The whole exercise has been fraught: when Lida offers to design the new letterhead a protest blows up among the staff. And always there is the regular everyday work schedule for the Workshop,

David started his Workshop in 1945; 50 years later after his death in 1995, it became the Cardozo Kindersley Workshop.

Chocolate letter K,
metal mould, given to
David by Gerard Unger
from Holland.

Gaynor Goffe gave
David this piece of
calligraphy she did
for him.

David Peace introduced
glass engraving to the
Workshop, and Mark
Bury, then apprenticed,
engraved the David
Kindersley design.

I am no more lonely than a single mullein or a dandelion in a pasture or a bean leaf or a sorrel or a horse fly or a humble bee I am no more lonely than the mill brook or a weather cock or the north star or the south wind or an April shower or a January thaw or the first spider in a new house

THOUGH I BE POOR, I'M HONEST.

John Benson's slate was part of a dual bet with David, for carving an inscription straight into stone without design or drawing out.

LE MAIUSCOLE
NON HANNO REGOLA
FERMA, SI FANNO A
GIUDITIO DELL'OCCHIO
COME QUI VEDETE

a summer exhibition in Holland where Lida is approached by someone about a new job, another conference in Lausanne for September/October...

Ah, Lausanne. It is clear in retrospect that David Kindersley was attracted to that Dutch girl nearly 40 years his junior from their first meeting in Poland. Her worship and understanding of his work must have been flattering too; so he took an absolutely determined stance of distancing himself from any involvement with her. He was a husband in a second troublesome marriage, he wanted to wind his activities down gently, and did not need new emotional entanglements. Nor would he have thought them proper.

Lida's persistence in making her way into his Workshop was a bafflement. He ran the place surrounded by 3 male assistants, with their own quirks and piques to exercise him. They were indeed fine craftsmen, working to a set routine with fixed hours – the master's instructions were there to be carried out, without question. The drive, enthusiasm and creative gifts of this young woman, entering this staid setting, must have been something

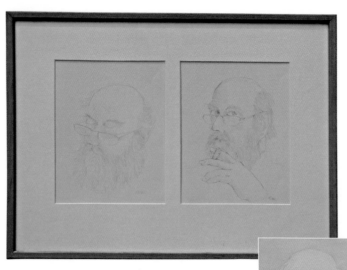

between a burst of sunlight and a thunderclap. During 1977 she became the engine that made the acquisition of, and then move to the Victorian schoolrooms a reality for the Workshop. And still he resisted, refusing very honourably to recognize a finger pointing from heaven.

That all changed with a knock on a hotel room's door in Lausanne one evening, Lida saying 'I really can't take this anymore'.

There are volumes of love letters between the two. For a year from November 1977 they wrote to each other almost daily, often in the small hours. Of course all best love letters blaze passion, touching the heights of carnal and spiritual longing, the impatience for the next meeting. And doubts here. Because during all that first year in the new Workshop, life had to

*David by Lida, on paper
and on a glass bottle.*

97

Lida by David in clay. David had been commissioned to do eight busts of 7/8 life size; he made this trial but found he was not at ease with the form. Lida, having to sit still, drew him at the same time.

continue as if nothing had happened in Lausanne. Not only was there the daily work of the master and his 4 staff; at night the master had to repair to his wife who was not well. What lit up the tender embrace of the lovers was the total conviction that they belonged to one another. Life was a tragic business, for sure. Companions-in-arms and lovers were God's only concessions, given very grudgingly, very rarely, and almost never together. They knew that.

David Kindersley was rejuvenated, no longer planning retirement but how to build a new future. His work with Lida also represented a fresh climb to new mountain tops. In time, the very real practical difficulties of sorting out a proper life together began to look less daunting – and even perhaps soluble.

At the beginning of 1979 Lida bought a house in Chesterton, and she and David could live together. They married in 1987.

David's former wife accepted the inevitable very graciously, acknowledging that she had never seen him so happy. Indeed relations between the three remained affectionate throughout. David continued to be concerned for Barbara and she outlived him.

Electricity isolator retrieved for Lida by Barbara's son from a telegraph pole.

Barbara Petrie as a young girl (signed P. B. J. 1930).

1979 was remarkable for a major Kindersley exhibition at the Amsterdam University Library in March/April. There was naturally much interest in the Dutch press: a 25 year old artist from The Hague joined up with a 64 year old Englishman! The show was a success; and so was something that pleased them greatly that year – writing 'Letters Slate Cut' together (first published 1981). Its dedication is to Harold Hunter, the lunch partner of their first Cambridge meeting.

Letters SLATE CUT: David and Lida's first publication together – see bibliography.

The EYE: 150·000·000 photoreceptors in the retina.

TRUMPINGTON STREET

Trumpington Street was the first attempt at a system for letter spacing.

OI IO

Take 01 - 10 of the alphabet: to be spaced as similar units.

OIIIO

Adjust the units until I looks in the middle.

OILIO

Adjust the units until 'L' looks in the middle. If there is space beyond that required for the 'L' reduce the spaces between 10 - 01 by that amount.

OIAIO

Now do the entire alphabet; but remember to mark the CENTRE on each letter. This is the centre between the two 'I's, & measure the space between the spaces allotted to the 'I's.

Showing how centres can be moved and spaces requirements reduced.

ABCDEFGHI
JKLMNOPQR
STUVWXYZ

All being carefully done any one letter will appear to be in the centre between its neighbours.

THE PROBLEM: How to find a mathematical progression that will give the centres as shown.

One of the many panels made for the Dutch exhibition.

The inscription carved in Dordrecht is by the Dutch poet Jan Eijkelboom: WAT BLIJFT KOMT NOOIT TERUG (What remains never comes back). Its very hard wearing stone is quarried in Belgium: Hardsteen, or Petit Granit (Belgian marble). The pair lived in the Netherlands for 3 weeks whilst cutting.

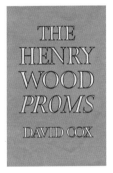

Book jackets for the BBC, commissioned by Charles Elton.

Wood letters cut out with a bandsaw for a panel at the then Cambridge Magistrates' Court (1980).

A third great 1979 venture was the 10' 6" (over 3 metres) long Welsh slate for the floor of St Albans Abbey, in front of the high altar. It covers the reinterred bones of the Abbey's abbots, and is fully described in 'Lasting Letters' (1992, see bibliography). You will find out there about its lettering influences, as well as why 'truth and understanding evolution walked hand in hand'. The whole design is dominated by the perspective of the viewer standing at the foot of the slab.

By 1984 Lida and David had been in a highly fruitful 7 year partnership. Love and work were a unity; they would wake up at night to say 'hey, that spacing – what do you think'. Indeed, letter spacing was an ever present concern, with Lida attending the University Computer Laboratory (1978–83, Dr Neil Wiseman). The trajectory of her work was steadily upward – and David's changed under her influence. She would say that she brought something of the purity of the plain Dutch landscapes to his florid English countryside. The outcome was a remarkable fusion of styles, most obviously in regard to their italic lettering. Of course they vied, and for a while travelled in lovely parallel. Seeing clients became a

65th birthday medal.

Traditionally glass is engraved with a diamond-tipped pencil; for an even texture a dentist's drill is used in the Workshop. When a number of glasses are to be done, the design can be sand-blasted.

Small things like this house number are of equal importance to the Workshop as the larger jobs – good care is taken of both.

joint task; they would share the driving there, the discussions, and the measuring up (in inches! Lida was metric). Followed by the design – and naturally there might be tensions. The work was always the only priority for David, and he could readily grow irritated if Lida's equally natural business sense bore in on a particular proposal. They could argue fiercely about their ideas.

The Workshop was still just the basic ground floor Victorian schoolroom, with offices partitioned off. In 1984 they decided on a grand extension, because Lida wanted to have children: they knew their partnership could not stand separation from their work. So the present structure of 152 Victoria Road was designed and built that year – an additional large new ground floor studio and ample living space above.

Slate blackboard in the Workshop – the saying is David's.

Three boys were born to the couple: Paul 1985, Hallam 1986, and Vincent 1988. Juggling parenthood and the Workshop had its trials, but they were not forbidding. The really serious blow came in the spring of 1987, when David fell ill. He spent 10 weeks in hospital. Lida had to take over running the Workshop all by herself, as well as tending two infants.

A wooden alphabet box was made for Paul who was born in 1985, followed by Hallam (1986) and Vincent (1988).

When the balcony was covered in, a new tile floor was commissioned from Margaret Angus (Maggie Berkowitz).

Workshop motto on a Welsh slate (31 × 46 cm).

This sundial was calculated and designed for Bellows Cottage, Buckinghamshire; but this smithy burnt down.

1844 1990

BELLOWS COTTAGE

SPELL is a green slate and a pun: a spelling mistake being anything but magic for a lettercutter.

This cast is from the Palombino marble portrait for Sir Philip Sidney in the crypt of St Paul's Cathedral – the original memorial burnt down in the Great Fire.

Flourished alphabet on glass roundel.

Brasses designed by the Workshop have traditionally been cut by metal engravers; they began in the 1940s with George Friend. These three are done by John Salt.

This book, acknowledging the benefactors of the libraries of Corpus Christi College, was placed here

D.D.
PEHIN DATO B.H.KHOO
K.J.TAN H.G.ANG 1965

This bookplate was sent after David's death by the Russian artist Boris Andreevich Tkachenko.

Kip Gresham silk-screened alphabet: one of a boxed set of 12, overlapping different alphabets.

The S is a sample of how to cut straight into plaster, for Emmanuel College, Cambridge.

PANTARHEI is 'Everything flows' (Heraclitus) – the surface of the Portland stone is masoned like a wave. This is a cast from it in the Workshop.

119

David's troubles were eventually diagnosed as giant cell arteritis. He returned home in the summer, set right again by steroids. But there was a subtle change in him. If the lettering paths of these two artisans were to be drawn as a graph, with a crossing point for their artistic endeavours, then the summer of 1987 was it. David never regained ascendancy, and a slow decline began to set in. The signs were very minor at first, for example messages or telephone numbers might be forgotten. He recognized his frailty.

This alphabet was the inspiration for the British Library gates.

David with Sir Colin St John Wilson on site at the British Library – the architect who commissioned the inscription. It was cut into the red sandstone above the entrance. What will go underneath, the Workshop wondered; no-one was sure. What about gates of really grand lettering? The committees liked that, and the present gates were designed by David & Lida.

THIS BUILDING
WAS OPENED BY
H[IS M]AJESTY THE [QU]EEN
[O]N 25 JU[NE] [20]03

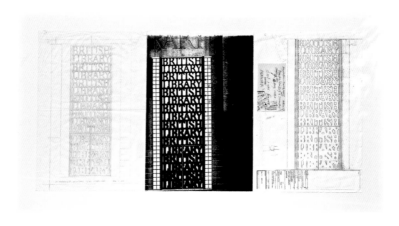

David and Lida's Workshop went on as before – though he did less, she more and more – until one day in September 1993. David was watching Lida doing drawing out on a stone, and said 'you know, you're much better than me – I'm stopping'. He

Portraits by James Horton (1994).

Unfinished carving of David by Lida.

kept to this sudden resolve, retiring
from creative work. He would still be
a strong presence in the Workshop,
encouraging the apprentices, pottering
about doing odd jobs – but no longer the master
in charge. He became increasingly forgetful.
There is a portrait of the couple by James Horton
that gives a wonderful glimpse into this period. David's look
is into the far distance, the
beyond. Richard Sword also
made a bust of him in 1994.

*David's head by
Richard Sword.*

He was taken very seriously
ill on 10 January 1995; a huge
bladder cancer was found, past
treatment. David Kindersley
died on 2 February 1995 – just 3
weeks later, and peacefully.

Goethe's poem in Welsh slate.

There is an inscribed slate bar on Lida's desk, carved by David in 1993. One side says 'The Workshop is dismantled after the work is finished'; the other 'You will know at the harvest that laziness is not planting'.

YOU WILL KNOW AT ᵗᴴᴱ HARVEST ᵗ ᴴ ᴬ ᵗ LAZINESS IS NOT PLANTING

The workshop is dismantled after the work is finished

David's death in 1995 marked a void. Lida's natural doubts about how to carry on were sharpened by the outside world regarding the Workshop as dismantled. The bank closed its accounts, and the Crafts Council erased its entry. David Kindersley was now history and his Workshop gone – it was thought.

There were some bright spots. Lida's task of looking after 3 children as well as the Workshop was eased by the arrival of Maryse Francois from Holland; she took over the boys. The accountant William Barnard tackled the Workshop's financial affairs with outstanding ability as well as sympathy: David's credo about 'the work first' was also his constant advice. And the highly experienced hospital administrator Graham Cannon joined the Workshop in order to supervise the apprentices. It was a tough job after 1995, but by the 2000 millennium the corner and void had been turned. Public and private commissions were streaming in once more: the new

A picture of Vincent Kindersley by his brother Paul.

Cardozo-Kindersley Workshop had taken off – a phoenix. And in 1998 Lida married Graham Beck, who had been engaged in administrative work for historic buildings and also heraldry. He took on the Workshop's business side, alongside Graham Cannon.

Millennium plate using Octavian (see page 69).

Graham Beck carved these initials in wood.

DAVID KINDERSLEY

An example of how David's street lettering became translated into transfer vinyl letters, and thus used for street names. A computer outlining typefaces would not have been approved by David; therefore Lida returned to his original drawing (see page 44) for computer developments such as the Grand Arcade lettering (see page 132).

Shingle Street is Lida & Graham's retreat on the Suffolk coast, with the film maker Tim Miller. She and Els Bottema laid a line of shells from the old coastguard house to the sea; it is a quiet place for gathering new strengths.

127

Shingle Street – one slate split into two halves;
quotation from William Blake:

And we are put on earth a little space,
    That we may learn to bear the beams of love.

Fibreglass bronze casts of carved slates, from Brian Scott McCarthy at the Wild Goose Studio. 'Yes Yes Yes' is a trivet.

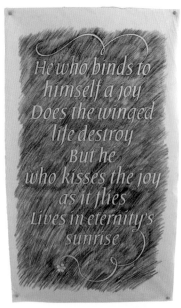

He who binds to
himself a joy
Does the winged
life destroy
But he
who kisses the joy
as it flies
Lives in eternity's
sunrise

Rubbing from the back of a gravestone.

The Tordoff Greek alphabet.

The Ornament of Bristol and the Wonder

'The Ornament of Bristol and the Wonder
of the Age. Isambard Kingdom Brunel
1806–1859': a brass commissioned by
Julia Elton for a 2006 competition on the
Clifton Suspension Bridge. Brunel used
novel suspension rods, hangers and links
– the basis of the design for this commem-
orative prize.

Remember
me
laughing

Slate roundel, quotation
from James Bradburne.

Today the Workshop is a busier place than ever, with the mistress, 3 each of lettercutters and apprentices, plus administrator/secretary/archivist staff. David Kindersley's inheritance is a weighty responsibility, shouldered here with much fun as well as seriousness. The harvest is as dependent on planting as ever (that inscription!), and there is no sense of treading water or merely copying past triumphs.

Age · Isambard Kingdom Brunel 1806–1859

The Workshop took a week out, with each member carving a head under the guidance of Bryn Ansell. Lida started on David (Portland stone).

ABCDEFG
HIJKLMN
OPQRSTU
VWXYZ &
abcdefghi
jklmnopq
rstuvwxyz
0123456789

In commemoration of the gift to Cambridge City Council of the licence to use
Kindersley Grand Arcade, commissioned from Lida Lopes Cardozo Kindersley
by the Universities Superannuation Scheme and Grosvenor in 2006

Lida Lopes Cardozo Kindersley

GRAND ARCADE

Grosvenor commissioned
Lida to digitize David's
original street lettering,
for the 2008 opening of
the Grand Arcade in
Cambridge. The original
was only in capitals, so
lower case and italic
letter forms had to be
designed in addition.
Eiichi Kono digitized the
typeface, which is now in
the public domain.

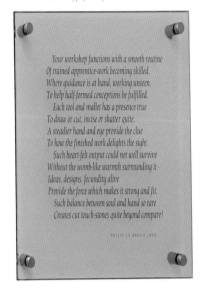

Your workshop functions with a smooth routine
Of trained apprentice-work becoming skilled,
Where guidance is at hand, working unseen,
To help half-formed conceptions be fulfilled.
　　Each tool and mallet has a presence true
To draw or cut, incise or shatter quite.
A steadier hand and eye provide the clue
To how the finished work delights the sight.
　　Such heart-felt output could not well survive
Without the womb-like warmth surrounding it -
Ideas, designs, fecundity alive
Provide the force which makes it strong and fit.
　　Such balance between soul and hand so rare
　　Creates cut touch-stones quite beyond compare!

PHILIP LE BROCQ 2008

Portland stone alphabet cut by various members of the
Workshop, as the basis of 'The Annotated Capital' (2009,
Cambridge University Press).

After all, innovation and development were essential to David Kindersley's achievement, and so it is now – alphabeticians cannot stand still. We glance back at our introduction, to the 'lettering man of the 20th century': his aspirations are in good hands for the 21st century.

TS

Every now and then Donald Simpson introduces new apprentices to carving in wood. Three trial pieces that encompass the Workshop.

WRITING & ILLUMINATING, & LETTERING.
Edward Johnston. 1917; London, John Hogg.

ART NONSENSE AND OTHER ESSAYS.
Eric Gill. 1929; London, Cassell & Co.

OPTICAL LETTER SPACING FOR NEW PRINTING SYSTEMS.
David Kindersley. 1st ed.1966, revised 1976 & 2001; Cambridge, Cardozo
Kindersley.

VARIATIONS ON THE THEME OF 26 LETTERS.
David Kindersley. 1969; Wellingborough, Skelton's Press.

GRAPHIC SAYINGS.
David Kindersley. 1972; Wellingborough, Skelton's Press.

LETTERS SLATE CUT.
David Kindersley & Lida Lopes Cardozo. 1st ed.1981, revised 1990 & 2004;
Cambridge, Cardozo Kindersley.

DAVID KINDERSLEY: HIS WORK AND WORKSHOP.
Montague Shaw. 1989; Cambridge, Cardozo Kindersley.

LASTING LETTERS.
Ed. Rosamond McKitterick & Lida Lopes
Cardozo Kindersley. 1992; Cambridge,
Cardozo Kindersley.

*The series of recent books from the
Cardozo Kindersley Workshop are listed
on the back cover flap.*

*Lottie Hoare would like to thank
the many individuals who through
sharing their memories of David
Kindersley helped tell the story of
the Workshop.*

WHEN
TOMORROW COMES,
THINK TOMORROW'S
THOUGHTS

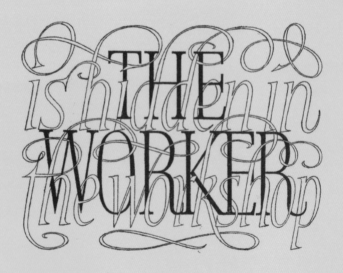

THE WORKER is hidden in the WORKSHOP